FIRE ON THE MOUNTAIN

FIRE ON THE MOUNTAIN

Sister Josephine and the Ark of the Covenant

BARBARA A. GASKELL

St. Raphael Center 4365 Fulton Dr NW Canton OH 44718

Contents

Dedication		vii
Introduction		ix
1	Sister Josephine	1
2	The Journey	6
3	Kiriath Yearim	10
4	The Land Purchase	12
5	Abu Gosh	14
6	The Discovery	16
7	The Construction	18
8	Final Days	22
9	The Ark in the Bible	27
10	Mary and the Ark	33
11	Modern Excavations	44
12	Marian Prayers	49
End Notes		59
About The Author		60

Copyright @ 2023 by **Barbara A. Gaskell**

All rights reserved. No part of this publication may be reproduced, distributed or transmitted in any form or by any means, without prior written permission.

All scripture quotes were taken from the New American Bible

St. Raphael Center, Inc.
4365 Fulton Drive N.W.
Canton, Ohio 44718

www.CatholicBook.net

First Printing, 2023

Fire on the Mountain/ Barbara A. Gaskell – 1st ed.
ISBN   978-1-7336090-2-9

This book is dedicated to Sister Josephine Rumebe, her love of Jesus Christ and the land where He walked while on earth has brought to our modern world an incredible gift that could have easily been lost to history. We owe a great debt to her strong determination and single-minded pursuit of God's will. May she be praising God in the New Jerusalem for all eternity.

Introduction

In 1998 I had the privilege of leading a wonderful group of pilgrims to the Holy Land. On the last day of our trip, my dear friend Suzanne, our spiritual advisor Fr. Gerald Sommer, M.S.C. and Maura, a pilgrim from New Jersey, and I rented a cab and visited the ancient village of Kiriath Yearim, now known as Abu Gosh.

This town, high at the top of the hill of Abinadab is the home of the Catholic Basilica, Notre-Dame-de-l'Arche-d'Alliance, or Mary, Ark of the Covenant. It is staffed by the Sisters of St. Joseph of the Apparition.

Fr. Gerald offered Mass for the Sisters and our little group in the church on this Holy Mountain that at one time was the most holy place in all the Israelite nation because it housed the Ark of the Covenant.

I

Sister Josephine

Jeanne Rumebe was born October 18, 1850 in the village of Aspet, France at the foot of the Pyrenees, sixty miles west of Lourdes and eight years prior to the Virgin Mary's visits to St. Bernadette. Jeanne was the fifth of six children in the family of Felix and Jeanne-Marie Rumebe.

Her grandparents had survived the French Revolution and her parents were both deeply religious. When Jeanne was nine her mother died. Only eight years later she experienced the death of her father. As well as being orphaned during her early years, Jeanne suffered poor health.

She was told by her mother and older sisters that the first word she spoke was "Jerusalem." By the time she was five she often said: "When I grow up, I will sell everything I own and I will have enough to go to Jerusalem where I want to live and die." *

(*"Cherubin sur la Colline de Dieu"* by Benoit Stoltz O.S.B. page 7)

When Jeanne was four, she began to be showered with extraordinary graces from Our Lord. She heard celestial voices and saw the baby Jesus in a field. When Jeanne was six, she had a vision of Jesus seated on his throne at the gate of paradise, surrounded by the apostles. At this incredible site she fell to the ground.

Jeanne shared all of her spiritual experiences with her mother who was kind and reflective. Jeanne remained hidden away in the family shed or under an apple tree for hours in solitary communion with Jesus. She engaged in extreme physical mortification and at the age of 14 offered herself to Jesus as a victim soul.

After her father's death, Jeanne was entrusted to her older brother, Michael. She had an overwhelming desire to enter the convent but her family tried every means to discourage her.

Jeanne enlisted the aid of a sympathetic sister and they devised a plan to make a pilgrimage to Lourdes but told the family they were to visit an aunt for several days. The two made the trip on foot with one franc between them. They begged for bread in the villages on the journey and arrived at Lourdes late at night. The two sisters spent the night in the Grotto during a torrential rain.

The next day was spent in intense prayer but as they were ready to leave Jeanne was discouraged that the Virgin Mary had not answered her prayers. The sisters used their franc to buy a few medals and a little bread for the return trip.

Upon leaving the Grotto they encountered a priest who asked them why they had visited Lourdes. The elder sister explained that they came to ask the Virgin Mary if Jeanne really had a religious vocation. The priest turned to Jeanne and said "You do have a religious vocation and you will enter the Sisters of St. Joseph of the Apparition in Marseilles where you will become the favorite daughter of Jesus. To St. Joseph! To St. Joseph! To St. Joseph!" he repeated.*
(*"Cherubin sur la Colline de Dieu"* by Benoit Stoltz O.S.B. page 15)

He then gave them enough money to take the train home and when they asked him to bless their medals, he said he did not have the power to do so. After their conversation he disappeared. The sisters stayed on another day to try to find him but to no avail. For the rest of her life Jeanne swore a solemn testimony that St. Joseph himself had appeared to them in Lourdes.

===============

The religious order of the Sisters of St. Joseph of the Apparition was founded by Blessed Emilie de Vialar in 1832 in Marseilles, France. Their foundress, who was still living, inspired her Sisters with a love for the Holy Land where in 1848, she opened a convent.

===============

When Jeanne returned from Lourdes and announced to her family that she wanted to enter the Sisters of St. Joseph of the Apparition her brother wrote to the Mother Superior and told her that Jeanne had always suffered from poor health and should not be admitted. But Jeanne was aided by a kindly doctor who gave her a good report.

In June of 1867, Jeanne's aunt and sister helped her escape to the train station when her brother Michael was away on a trip. She took a train to Marseilles where Sister Emilie had established the Motherhouse and asked to be admitted.

When her brother later threatened to come and take her home by force, she agreed to his wishes but said she would die of grief. Finally, her family relented, and they reconciled with Jeanne sometime later.

During her novitiate, Jeanne, like other novices, had to perform household chores and farm yard jobs like milking cows. She was not accomplished at farm work and on one occasion, while feeding the pigs, she left the sty door open, and the animals got out. She called aloud on her patron St. Joseph. The gardener, who fortunately had the same name, heard her cry, and came to her rescue.

The Mistress of Novices, while recognizing her goodness, said that if she ever did anything worthwhile it would be the work of God. She told the Mother Superior that sending Jeanne Rumebe to the missions would be a waste of money.

The Sisters gradually became aware of her claims of apparitions and visions in her early years though most were skeptical. One day during her novitiate while in prayer, she gazed on Jesus in the Blessed Sacrament and she then saw a mountain ablaze and on top of it stood Jesus, dazzlingly bright. His arms were open as if to say, "Come." He shone in all His glory. Unable to bear the brilliance. She dropped her eyes, and when she looked up again it had disappeared. Overcome with joy she wept. Fifty-six years later when she was extremely ill, she confided this vision to a priest and said that even in the face of death, she would stand firm that it was all true.

After a rigorous novitiate, Jeanne, at the age of 18, professed her vows, taking the name of Sister Josephine. Shortly afterwards she left for Jerusalem, her Mistress of Novices still doubtful about her capabilities. This was for Sister Josephine the beginning of a love relationship with the Holy Land which was to last for almost 60 years.

Sr. Josephine Rumebe
Sisters of St. Joseph of the Apparition

2

The Journey

JERUSALEM

Although she had an aversion to the sick and dying, Sister Josephine spent the first five years in Palestine as a nursing aide in the Jerusalem hospital which the Sisters of St. Joseph of the Apparition had started in 1851. During that time the infant mortality rate was high due to poor sanitation and hygiene.

Sister Josephine cared for the many impoverished families in the region by supplying not only medical help but more importantly she gave instructions in the faith and baptized many dying souls.

On one occasion during a terrible epidemic Sister Josephine baptized twelve dying children in one day on the city streets. As she and another Sister made their way home they found a child near death in his mother's arms. To her dismay Sister Josephine's holy water bottle was empty. A young man approached them and handed her a goblet filled with water. His face shone with such beauty that she was dumbfounded. Sister Josephine took the goblet and baptized the baby, immediately the baby died. Upon turning to thank the young man he had disappeared. Sister Josephine was convinced that St. Joseph himself had come to her rescue.

CYPRUS

In 1874 Sister Josephine answered a call for help during a cholera epidemic that was sweeping through Cyprus where the Sisters had been working for 30 years. She immersed herself in the work and after three years she fell victim to cholera. She went into a coma and her doctor said she would never recover. To all appearances she stopped breathing, but Sister Josephine was miraculously cured by Jesus through a heavenly encounter with Sister Marie of Jesus Crucified. After she recovered, she said that Sister Marie reassured her that she would not die as God had plans for her in the Holy Land.

Saint Marie Jesus Crucified

RETURN TO JERUSALEM

In January 1877 Sister Josephine left Cyprus for Jaffa where for several years she supervised the building of extensions to the sisters' hospital. Upon completion of the project, she returned to her beloved Jerusalem.

During this time, Count Amedee de Piellat, a French aristocrat came to Jerusalem, who as a young man had become, like Sister Josephine, enamored by the Holy Land. He decided to devote himself to the care of places of Christian interest and to providing a better hospital for the Sisters work. He purchased a place just outside the Old City's walls, called by the Arabs, Place of the Terebinth. This name was given because of a nearby tree. While the new hospital was being erected, the Sisters set up a provisional dispensary under the Terebinth's shade.

As well as building St. Louis Hospital which opened in 1879, Count de Piellat arranged many pilgrimages that came from France. The imposing Notre Dame de France Hotel opened in 1887. Before then the Count had to arrange itineraries and accommodations for the French pilgrims at a time when travel was rigorous and hazardous. He enlisted the services of Sister Josephine as the traveling nurse, and she became a familiar sight, mounted on a horse, braving exhaustion and the dangers of primitive travel. Often the groups would spend ten or twelve hours a day visiting the holy sites.

Sister Josephine attended to the pilgrims' needs with her mobile dispensary treating various types of illness, dressing wounds, setting broken limbs, and dealing with sunstroke. More importantly she valued the opportunity to lead souls into a deeper relationship with her Savior, Jesus Christ. On many occasions, she brewed her famous herbal tea, which the pilgrims said had healing properties. It earned her the nick name Sister Camomile.

Sister Josephine also became closely acquainted with the other religious orders and Congregations coming to Palestine. She helped several buy property and establish monasteries there. Among her close friends were the Cistercians of Latroun who came in 1890, and the Benedictine Monks who came from the monastery of La Pierre-qui-vive in 1901.

These Benedictines began to restore a magnificent crusader church about 11 miles from Jerusalem in a village named after a well-known bandit, Abu Ghosh. The hill above Abu Ghosh was known as Kiriath Yearim (the town of the forest) or Kiriath el' Enab (the town of the grass) and its summit was called Der-el-Azhar, which means the Convent of Flowers. This was significant in the light of later events.

In 1901 the Mother General of the Sisters of St. Joseph of the Apparition was passing through Jerusalem. The Father Superior of the Benedictines invited her to spend the day in Kiriath Yearim with them. She accepted the Benedictine hospitality and Sister Josephine arranged the trip in a two-horse carriage. Later in the day they climbed to the summit of Kiriath Yearim. Reverend Mother was delighted with the magnificent panorama. The vistas from the top of the mountain were unparalleled.

Before leaving Jerusalem, the Mother General called together the entire Community of St. Louis Hospital and said, "I have thought about it carefully and I would like us to buy Kiriath Yearim. I know Sister Josephine and I charge her with this foundation. I give her full permission and I want Kiriath Yearim's fund to be separate from the Hospital's." * *"Cherubin sur la Colline de Dieu"* by Benoit Stoltz O.S.B. page 56

3

Kiriath Yearim

It is important to note that the Biblical significance of the site of Kiriath Yearim was not lost on the Mother General or other Catholic leaders in the Holy Land.

In 1901, the entire area was ruled by a Muslim Sheik Abdullah who had no interest in Jewish or Christian history.

The first book of Samuel recounts how the Philistines captured the Ark of the Covenant in a rout of the Israelites. When the Philistines housed the Ark in the temple of their god, Dagon they began to experience terrible calamities.

The area was overrun by mice and all the people suffered greatly. Those that didn't die had boils and tumors on their bodies. There was terror throughout the city. For seven months the Philistines suffered while the Ark was in their presence.

The Philistines decided to send the Ark back to the Israelites. They placed the Ark on a cart and had two young cows pull it. They sent messages to the men of Kiriath Yearim to come and meet the cart. The men came down to get it and took it to the house of Obededum on the Hill of Abinidab. The Ark of the Covenenat remained there for almost 100 years until King David took it to a permanent home in the Temple of Jerusalem. The hill of Abinidab is also known as Kiriath Yearim.   (See 2 Samuel chapter 6)

Kiriath Yearim
Bibleplaces.com

4

The Land Purchase

Sister Josephine approached the Father Superior of the Peres Blancs, or White Fathers to ask for help in purchasing the land. Brother Louis was put at her disposal. He had business experience and had acquired several parcels for his own community.

A French cousin had sent Sister Josephine 5000 gold francs, which she hid under a loose floor tile in her bedroom. She told Brother Louis, "Listen carefully, I have only 5000 francs. Do not exceed that sum. Try to acquire the upper half of the hill and the part near the Benedictine convent." (*"Cherubin sur la Colline de Dieu"* by Benoit Stoltz O.S.B. page 57)

Brother Louis traveled to see Sheikh Abdulla to make the purchase but he encountered an official from the German Consulate who was also intent on purchasing land there. The official had already agreed to purchase several plots on the east side. Brother Louis decided to disregard Sister Josephine's warning and negotiated for the property she wanted. Contracts were established and signed by Brother Louis and the Sheikh.

When the day of payment arrived Brother Louis presented Sister Josephine with the list of acquired parcels and a bill totaling 20,732 francs. Sister Josephine was astounded, reminding him that she had said not to exceed 5,000 francs. He explained that he was afraid the official from the German Consulate would buy up everything.

Sister Josephine went to her bedroom to retrieve the hidden 5,000 francs to make an installment payment on the total. Upon counting out the francs she found that she had 20,732 francs, the exact amount needed. Stunned she went to get another Sister to recount the coins and Sister Lucy counted 20,732 francs.

Sister Josephine certified the miraculous multiplication of the gold coins on a purchase note kept in the archives. Many times Sister Josephine told the Sisters, "Graces and blessings that once accompanied the Ark of the Covenant are still here."*

("Cherubin sur la Colline de Dieu"* by Benoit Stoltz O.S.B. page 58)

5

Abu Gosh

After the land purchase was completed Sister Josephine took up residence in Abu Gosh. It was an extremely harsh environment both physically and politically. Abu Gosh was named for a powerful Muslim military family that ruled the area from the 16th century onward. They were feared throughout the region for their ruthless treatment of travelers who did not pay them tribute. At one time they controlled twenty-two villages.

The terrain was harsh with no other access but an uneven, stony path. The summit was overgrown, home to jackals, snakes and hyenas. It was in this hostile environment that Sister Josephine pitched her tent. She entrusted herself completely to God's Providential care.

Monsieur Bopp who was the French Consul to Jerusalem, made it well know that Sister Josephine was under the direct protection of the French Government.

Sister Josephine put together a small dispensary near the Benedictine monastery. Soon the poor residents of the surrounding villages began to visit her for medical help. She was an indefatigable missionary, one day treating more than 90 patients. Any gifts she received she distributed to the poor.

One woman who visited Sister Josephine had a withered hand. Sister used the local spring water and a blessing, wrapped it, and sent her home. The next day the woman returned overjoyed. She was completely healed!

The hostility of the villagers gave way to respect and trust. Sheikh Abdulah promised to take Sister Josephine under his personal protection.

While devoting herself to the poor, Sister built a little house. She began to clear the land for a garden to support the convent. She employed local villagers and wrote correspondence to her benefactors in France to raise the funds for payment of wages and materials.

With her benefactors' support she was able to purchase another parcel of land. She requested that one of the priests celebrate Mass on the site and she had him consecrate the land to the Sacred Heart, beseeching Jesus to take possession of the land she had acquired for Him.

6

The Discovery

A local workman clearing brush discovered a line of huge ancient stones. Further digging uncovered colored mosaic tiles and sculpted stones forming the foundation of a large church. The church was surrounded by small cells for the guardians of the sanctuary and twelve cisterns hewn into the rock. It was the remains of a Byzantine Basilica and convent erected about 450 A.D. The nearby inhabitants had named it the "basilica of the flowers."

It had been built on the site of the Old Testament "high place" which had very early on become a Christian center of worship. Scholars were convinced that the Christians had built the basilica there to honor an old tradition which is enshrined in Psalm 131:

> *At Ephrata we heard of the Ark,*
> *We found it in the plains of Yearim.*

They believed that this spot, Kiriath Yearim, was one of the most hallowed places in the history of the Old Testament because the

Ark of the Covenant, the most precious possession of the Jews, had rested here for nearly a century before it was taken up to Jerusalem by King David.

The Byzantine Basilica had been looted and destroyed in the Persian occupation of 614 A.D. It was later rebuilt but destroyed again in 1010 by Hakam Kalife. For centuries after, the site was left desolate until Sister Josephine arrived to rescue it from oblivion.

According to a Greek-Palestinian liturgical calendar of the seventh century, July 2nd was recorded as the Feast of the Ark of the Covenant. Catholic Church writings show that a basilica was built in Kiriath Yearim around 444-460 AD because the first Christians wanted to consecrate the memory of the "dwelling of God." They believed this is where the Ark of the Covenant rested.

7

The Construction

Sister Josephine made plans to build a church, a convent and a dispensary on the property. In May of 1911, Sister Josephine invited the Latin Patriarch of Jerusalem, Bishop Camassei, to bless the cornerstone of the new convent.

The blessing was a great event. It was attended by the Consul General of France and his entourage, the Father General of the Franciscans, the Prior of the Trappists, the Superior of the Benedictine Fathers, the Assumptionists, the White Fathers, the Brothers of Christian Schools, and all the Sisters of St. Joseph in the surrounding area.

After the blessing, the Latin Patriarch, trembling with emotion, confided to Sister Josephine that during his blessing he saw the entire area covered with a multitude of angels in joyous adoration.

Within a year the convent was completed and furnished. A steady stream of donations kept the workers paid. The pharmacy quickly followed.

Our Lord told Sister Josephine a chastisement of the world was coming that would force her to leave and when she returned there would be nothing left but a wooden bench.

In 1914, at the beginning of World War I all French nationals were expelled from Palestine and ordered to return to France. Sister Josephine prayed especially to Our Lady for protection of the buildings before leaving. She placed a Lourdes statue on a table in the entry way. Then she and 66 Sisters of St. Joseph of the Apparition sailed to France on December 25, 1914.

They returned to France where they tended the wounded and dying. Meanwhile, Sister Josephine renewed contact with influential people who had already helped her and who would continue to help her in Jerusalem.

During these years in France, Sister Josephine wrote to her friends and benefactors a short and very eloquent account of Kiriath Yearim:

"I want to speak to you of the Holy Mountain and you will perhaps be surprised to hear me say that this was the first sanctuary in the world. Yes, here at Kiriath Yearim of the Bible, the Ark of the Covenant, the Holy of Holies, came to rest after its sojourn at Shiloh for 80 years. Nazareth and Bethlehem did not exist, nor did Calvary and the Holy Sepulcher. There was not even a temple at Jerusalem when the Holy of Holies dwelt on this Holy Mountain. To this place came the holy King David to take the Ark of the Covenant and to bring it, as the Scriptures tell us, to Jerusalem. Here it is that he began his canticle of love as he danced before the Ark.

"Under God's orders Moses had constructed a mobile tent tabernacle of which the most sacred part was the Holy of Holies in which was placed the Ark of the Covenant. The Ark of the Covenant was overshadowed by a luminous cloud which moved with it and accompanied the Israelites in the desert; for them it opened a passage through the Jordan. It gave them

victory over their enemies and assured their conquest of the Holy Land. Then after a period among the Philistines, it came to rest for almost a century on the Holy Mountain among the people of Kiriath Yearim. And then it waited for David to build it a sanctuary shrine on Mount Sion, and for the magnificent temple Solomon would build for it in stone.

"The Holy Mountain is the mountain of blessings. There you have the Ark of the Covenant and the treasures it contained: the holy manna that fell from the sky, the rod of Aaron which blossomed miraculously. There you have the Holy of Holies and God enthroned above two cherubim who lie prostrated before Him and hide from His majesty behind their wings. The overwhelming presence – almost tangible – of the one true God in this place, unique in all the world." (Sisters of St. Joseph of the Apparition)

Her lyricism contrasted starkly with the reality she had to face when she returned to Kiriath Yearim in 1919. She found the place in ruins and even the statue of Our Lady of Lourdes, which she had left behind, although intact, was booby-trapped. But undaunted, she set to work again, determined to erect a new sanctuary worthy of this holy place.

On January 8, 1920, the foundation stone of the new sanctuary was laid by Cardinal Dubois, Archbishop of Paris. He dedicated the future basilica to the Blessed Virgin Mary under the title, "Our Lady Arche D'Alliance. The translated parchment reads "Our Lady of the Ark of the Covenant, to the Blessed Virgin Mary, symbolized by the Ark of the Old Covenant." After the ceremony the Cardinal knelt and lead a rosary invoking Our Lady, Ark of the Covenant." It was a title already used in the Litany of the Blessed Virgin Mary.

During the blessing of the cornerstone Sister Josephine was given to understand the vision she had seen 50 years earlier of the fire on the mountain and Jesus in all his brilliance beckoning her to come.

****

A French widow, Madame Revoil, who had already given one daughter, Anais, to the Sisters of St. Joseph, came with her other daughter Marie-Julie (who was to join the Congregation) to live and work with the poor in Abu Gosh. They did the mosaic work on the sanctuary of the church. Later, Madame Revoil's son Joseph was ordained a priest in the Sanctuary of Mary, Ark of the New Covenant.

During Holy Week in 1922 Sister Josephine had a vision of the Blessed Mother radiating her graces to the entire world. A statue was later completed and erected above the basilica. It depicts Our Lady facing Jerusalem, offering Jesus to the whole world.

At last, on August 31, 1924, the great day of the consecration of the sanctuary dedicated to Mary Ark of the New Covenant arrived. It was almost 25 years since Sr. Josephine had taken up her lonely watch on the hill. Pope Pius XI sent a telegram of blessing and Monsignor Barlassina, the Patriarch of Jerusalem, came with his entourage to perform the ceremony.

All the religious orders were represented at the august event, along with the Consul of France, his staff and several other foreign consuls. Four hundred people attended the feast following the ceremony. It was the culmination of Sister Josephine's life work. Our Lord revealed to her that this Basilica would be more pleasing to Him than the Temple of Solomon.

8

Final Days

From 1923 onwards, Sister Josephine experienced some very heavy crosses. She wrote of searing torture in her body and stabbing pains that made her feel as though she was being cut by a knife. She wrote also of the deep spiritual anguish during which she could not pray and seemed abandoned by God. Sometimes she bent in agony and cried aloud, especially in the night. A Sister who spent long vigils in the same room to comfort her, preferred not to speak of the terrible seizures and temptations Sister Josephine had to undergo.

Sister Josephine spent her last years in Kiriath Yearim. In 1925 she lost two of her closest friends. One was Count Amadee de Piellat, who died at the Hospital of St. Louis which had been largely his own work. The other was Father Pel, who helped her and had been her devoted spiritual director while she was in France.

At the end, Sister Josephine spent long hours looking towards Jerusalem which she could see clearly in the distance and meditating on the New Jerusalem she was about to enter. This she did – after prolonged sufferings – on September 1, 1927, just three years after the consecration of the Basilica. Her last words, spoken to Fr. Joseph Revoil, were: "I am with Christ who has never forsaken me." * (Sisters of St. Joseph of the Apparition)

Sister Josephine's grave in the church

Church of the Ark of the Covenant

Statue on top of the church

FIRE ON THE MOUNTAIN - 25

Interior of Church with ancient mosaic floor
Mosaic floor circa 200 AD

Ancient rock with Roman inscriptions unearthed by Sister Josephine
Circa 250 AD

9

The Ark in the Bible

The central message of the Bible both in the Old and New Testaments is the "Abiding and Saving Presence of God among men." In the Old Testament this Presence is often localized at "high places" and altars and sanctuaries, but above all in the Temple – and the Ark of the Covenant.

To understand this, one must go back to the desert days of the Israelites when they were a nomadic tribe who, like all nomadic tribes, regarded certain places as being places of religious interest. These they honored with stone monuments or altars, but the place more honored than all others was what they called the Tent of Meeting or the Tent of the Covenant. It was to grow later into their Temple, and its central feature was the Ark of the Covenant.

The Meeting Tent was, as its name suggests, the place where God and man met. And they met there because of the Covenant which God had made with Abraham, Isaac and Jacob. This covenant would be renewed, restored and ratified throughout their history.

In its original form the Meeting Tent was pitched in a "courtyard," or rectangular area cordoned and cut off from the outside by four walls of curtains. The entrance to the Tent itself led to the Holy Place which the priests could enter. Then once a year the High Priest, and only the High Priest, went from the (larger) Holy Place into the (much smaller) Holy of Holies where the Ark of the Covenant was kept.

Old Testament Meeting Tent

The Ark was the focal point of Israel's life. Materially it was a wooden box measuring approximately 49¼" x 29½" x 29½", and contained the two tablets of the Law which were believed to have come down from Mosaic times. According to a tradition recorded in the Letter to the Hebrews (9:4), it also contained some of the manna from the desert and the rod of Aaron, which blossomed miraculously. But the most important feature of the Ark was the Kapporet: a flat slab of gold on the top of the Ark, shaded or "overshadowed" by the wings of two carved cherubim, one on either side. It was known as the "mercy seat" or the "propitiatory" or the "Seat of Yahweh" who "rode on the wings of the cherubim."

The Ark of the Covenant

When the Israelites traveled through the desert, the Ark was carried in front of them by pole bearers and it led their army into battle. They carried it before them across the Jordan, and for seven days around Jericho before this key city fell. Eventually it was established in Shiloh.

But the Philistines who defeated Israel captured the Ark and took it away with them. They came to regret their trophy, however, because they were devastated by an earthquake which brought the statue of their great god Dagon crashing down at Ashdod. Plagues also broke out wherever they took the Ark – in Ashdod, Gad and Ekron. Deciding to rid themselves of it, they put the Ark into an ox-cart, and with great relief sent the oxen off to the Israelites at Bethshemesh.

From the ABC Parish

The inhabitants of Bethshemesh also were struck by a plague. Then the men of Bethshemesh said, "*Who can stand his ground before Yahweh this holy God; to whom shall we let him go up, away from us.*" So they sent messengers to the inhabitants of Kiriath Yearim, saying, *The Philistines have sent back the Ark of Yahweh; come down and take it up to your own town.* The men of Kiriath Yearim came and taking up the ark of Yahweh took it to the house of Abinadab on the hill. (1 Sam. 6:19) After their defeat by the Philistines and the plague at Bethshemesh, the Israelites were fearful of the Ark and it remained in Kiriath Yearim for almost 100 years.

Eventually David, who was trying to unite a fragmented people, thought the Ark could be instrumental in gathering the people together. So he took it to his newly conquered city, Jerusalem. Later it went into battle against Ammon, and finally came to settle in the Temple built by David's son Solomon. We hear no more about the Ark in the historical books of the Bible, but there are poetical echoes of it in some of the Psalms.

The Second Book of Maccabees (2:5) quotes a tradition that the prophet Jeremiah saved it and hid it with other precious things on Mt. Nebo where it was to remain undiscovered until Yahweh gathered his people together again. It is most probable that it was destroyed with the Temple in 587 B.C. Jeremiah himself, speaking to his people, said:

> And when you have increased and become many in the land – it is Yahweh who speaks – no one will ever say again, 'Where is the ark of the Covenant of Yahweh?' There will be no thought of it, no memory of it, no regret for it, no making of another.

The Book of Revelation fittingly has the final word. We are introduced there to a vision where 24 elders, enthroned in God's presence, prostrate themselves, touch the ground with their foreheads worshipping God, and cry: *We give thanks to you almighty Lord God, for using your great power and beginning to reign.* Then the text goes on to say:

> *The sanctuary of God in heaven opened, and the Ark of the Covenant could be seen inside it. Then came flashes of lightning, peals of thunder, and an earthquake, and violent hail. And there appeared a great wonder in heaven; a woman clothed with the sun, and the moon under her feet, and upon her head a crown of twelve stars:* **(Revelation 11-12)**

Mary, Ark of the Covenant window
St. Raphael Center, Inc. Canton, Ohio

10

Mary and the Ark

OLD TESTAMENT

The word of Yahweh came to Nathan (the prophet); Go and tell my servant David, "Thus Yahweh speaks: Are you the man to build me a house to dwell in?

I have never stayed in a house from the day I brought the Israelites out of Egypt until today, but have always led a wanderer's life in a tent.... In all my journeying with the whole people of Israel." (2 Samuel 7:5-7)

When St. John wished to describe the way in which God became man in order to become our Emmanuel – our God with us – he used a very striking phrase saying that the Word was made flesh and pitched his tent among us. (Jn 1:14) In Israel, Bedouin nomads still pitch their tents as they move from place to place. They are a pilgrim people living with all the insecurity and suffering that pilgrimage involves. And so too are the people of God in their exile. The Christian Church originated in the nomadic tent of the desert and – as St. Paul tells us – we do not have here a lasting city, but we seek one that is to come. During the days of its pilgrimage, the Church looks to Mary, Ark of the New Covenant, as its model. Vatical II spoke of her as the pilgrim "par excellence." She who herself walked the journey of life in an exemplary way is now our inspiration.

Mary is also an inspiration for the Church as she, like the Ark, was the repository of God's presence and holiness. In the case of the Ark this idea is expressed in Scripture by symbols which are extremely rich in meaning and often woven together in a way that defies analysis. The most important of these symbols is the Cloud, or Shekinah Glory. The Cloud did remarkable things: it stood immobile at the entrance to the Tent of Meeting; it led the Hebrews to freedom out of Egypt; it covered Mt. Sinai when Moses climbed up to converse with God; it filled the Temple so that no one could enter it. It revealed the Splendor of Yahweh and emphasized that the Ark of the Covenant was the intimate center of God's abiding Presence.

Moses and Joshua bowing before the Ark of the Covenant
(c 1900) by James Tissot

NEW TESTAMENT

To understand the relationship between the Ark of the Covenant and Mary, it will help to look at the many parallels between the Old Testament and the New. For example, here is the parallel between the Canticle of Hanna (1 Sam. 1) and the Canticle of Mary (Luke 2):

THE CANTICLE OF HANNA
My heart hath rejoiced in the Lord
I have joy in thy salvation.
There is none as holy as the Lord.
The bow of the mighty is overcome and the weak are girt with strength.
They that were full before have
Hired themselves out for bread; and the hungry are filled.
The Lord ... humbleth and he exalteth.

THE CANTICLE OF MARY
My soul magnifies the Lord,
and my spirit rejoices in God my savior.
Holy is his name.
He has shown might with his arm
He has scattered the proud in the conceit of their heart.
He has filled the hungry with good things and the rich he has sent away empty.
He has put down the mighty from their thrones, and has exalted the lowly.

COMPARISON

ARK: The Holy Spirit overshadowed the Ark. The Ark became the dwelling place of the presence of God. Exodus 40: 34-35

MARY: The Holy Spirit overshadowed the Virgin Mary and her womb became the dwelling place of the presence of God. Luke 1:35

ARK: The Ark contained the tablets of the Ten Commandments, a pot of manna and Aaron's rod that blossomed miraculously.

MARY: The womb of Mary contained Jesus, the "Lawgiver," the Bread of Heaven and she was a Virgin who blossomed miraculously.

ARK: The Ark traveled to the hill country of Judah to stay in the house of Obededom.   2 Samuel 6:1-11

MARY: Mary traveled to the hill country of Judah to stay in the house of Elizabeth. Luke 1:35

ARK: King David danced and leaped before the Ark with joy. 2 Samuel 6-14

MARY: John the Baptist leaped in his mother Elizabeth's womb as the Virgin Mary approached.   Luke 1:43

ARK: David asked, "How is it that the Ark of the Lord comes to me?" 2 Samuel 6-9

MARY: Elizabeth askes, "How is it that the Mother of my Lord comes to me?" Luke 1:43

This parallel, as well as many others like it, shows that the Old Testament is living in the New Testament. St. Augustine was so impressed by the way in which the Old Testament foreshadowed Christ, that he compared it to a mother in labor, saying it was pregnant with Christ.

Vatican II echoed his words when in reference to Mary, it said: "The long waiting for the promise is finally over, the ages are brought to completion with the surpassing Daughter of Sion." The Church of the Old Testament was the Church of great expectations, and it reached the term of its confinement in the person of a Virgin Mother who brought forth her first-born in Bethlehem and laid him in a manger. Together these two, Mother and Son, are the culmination of the prophecies, the realization of ancient hopes and dreams. Here in reality are the Woman and her offspring spoken of in Genesis, the Virgin and her child predicted by Isaiah.

Popes and bishops as well as Scripture scholars and theologians have written copiously of Mary in the light of the Bible, from which they have drawn many rich titles to describe her. Among these titles perhaps the richest is Mary, Ark of the New Covenant. The idea of Mary as the Ark of the New Covenant springs mainly from the fact that the Angel Gabriel addresses her in words that are found repeatedly in the "annunciation" to the people of Israel in other places in the Bible, and these are always announcements of the Good News that God will dwell among men. Notice, for example, the similarities between the "annunciation" in Zephaniah and Luke:

ZEPHANIAH 3
Shout for Joy
Rejoice, exult
Daughter of Zion
Daughter of Jerusalem
Yahweh your God is in your midst

LUKE 1
Rejoice
So highly favored
The Lord is with you.
Do not be afraid.
Mary, you are to conceive and bear a son and you must name him Jesus (Yoshia)
Have no fear Zion
Yahweh your God is in your midst
A victorious warrior (Yoshia)

In the Annunciation, Mary is the personification of her people, Israel, to whom – once more – the Good News is addressed, this time through her. Through Mary, God will become present to us in a new and wondrous way. And just as the Cloud is described in Exodus as overshadowing the Tent of Meeting which housed the Ark, so too, using the same word, the Angel tells Mary: *The Holy Spirit will come upon you and the Most High will overshadow you.*

Pope Paul VI pointed out that the early Church Fathers reflected on this text and on the fact that Mary, "overshadowed" by the Most High, became the repository not simply of the tablets of the Law, but of the Law-giver Himself; not simply of the desert manna, but of the Living Bread from heaven. Hence, they called her by such titles as Abode of the King, Tabernacle of the Lord, Ark of Holiness, and Ark of the Covenant. (1974 Encyclical Maria Cultus)

Paul VI drew attention to other parallels between the Old and New Testaments concerning the Visitation. David cried out as the Ark was being taken up to Jerusalem: *How can the ark of Yahweh come to me?* And Elizabeth cried out as Mary came to her: *How is it that the mother of my Lord should come to me?* As David danced before the Ark, so the child in Elizabeth's womb leapt for joy. And as the

Ark was left by David in the house of Abinadab for three months, bringing it a blessing, so Mary brought a blessing to the house of Zachary and Elizabeth where she too stayed for three months. Mary is indeed the "Mother of my Lord," an honorific title in the Old Testament by virtue of her being the Ark of the New Covenant.

Closely linked to these titles is Mary, Spouse of Yahweh, again harking back to the Old Testament theme that Yahweh had wooed His people as a lover and through His overshadowing of her took possession of her and made her His Bride. In the same way, He takes Mary who conceives His Son by the power of the Holy Spirit. The idea of Yahweh's overshadowing is expressed in a similar way by Ezekiel who uses a Hebrew custom to describe Yahweh's marriage with Israel:

Then I saw you as I was passing. Your time had come, the time for love. I spread part of my cloak over you... I bound Myself by oath, I made a covenant with you – And you became mine. (Ezekiel 16:18)

Likewise, the cherubim bowing down over the Ark and hiding their faces in a posture of awe and adoration before Yahweh reflect many passages in the Bible where angelic hosts bow down before Him and cry "Holy, Holy, Holy, Lord God of Hosts."

In the same way, Mary in her Immaculate Conception stands out as uniquely exemplifying the holiness of God. Vatican Council II says: "Enriched from the first instant of her conception with the splendor or an entirely unique holiness, the virgin of Nazareth is hailed by the heralding angel, by divine command, as full of grace." The title "Immaculate" which we apply to Mary should not be thought of negatively; we say she is Immaculate not simply because she had no sin, original or actual, but because positively, she is full of holiness, full of grace. She is the Inmost Shrine, the Holy of Holies overshadowed by the Cloud of the Holy Spirit and encompassing in her very body the Holy One Himself. As Pope

Paul VI said, she is the Ark of Holiness, beckoning each one of us to strive in our turn for holiness of life.

The old Ark, as the symbol of God's holiness, was the center of liturgical worship and glorious celebration. When it was being borne solemnly into Jerusalem to the great joy of the people:

David danced, whirling round before Yahweh with all his might, wearing a linen loincloth round him. Thus, David and all the House of Israel brought up the Ark of Yahweh with acclaim and the sound of the horn. (2 Samuel 6:14-23)

Psalm 23 very likely describes this procession with the ritual entry of the Ark:

O gates lift high your heads, grow higher ancient doors; Let him enter the King of glory. Who is he, the King of glory? He, the Lord of armies, He is the King of glory.

This entry of the Ark into Jerusalem paved the way for another great feast which, after the building of the temple, became the high point of the Jewish liturgical year. Once a year on the feast of Yom Kippur (Day of Atonement) the High Priest entered the Holy of Holies where he sprinkles the blood of animals on the Kapporet of the Ark to make the intercession for his people.

The Letter to the Hebrews (chapter 9) uses this once-yearly event to describe another great event – the Ascension of Our Lord. It speaks of the Ascension in terms of the high Priest going into the Holy of Holies on Yom Kippur, the Day of Expiation. It says that Christ in His Ascension now "goes up" as our great High Priest and enters once and for all into Heaven, the Holy of Holies, the "place of rest," where He continues to make intercession for us.

On the feast of the Assumption, the Church sees Mary as going to join her Son. As the Ark of Holiness, she enters with Him into Heaven, the place of her rest too, and there with Him she continues her intercession on our behalf.

The first reading of the Vigil Mass for the feast of the Assumption tells appropriately of David bringing the ark from Shiloh to give it a resting place in the tent at Jerusalem. When one remembers that Mary, as well as being the Ark of the Covenant is also the Daughter of Sion, the Responsorial Psalm (in which the whole church responds to God's message) is seen to be very fitting (Ps. 132). In the context of the Assumption, it is exceptionally rich in symbolism:

> *At Ephrata we heard of the Ark,*
> *we found it in the plains of Yearim.*
> *Go up Lord to the place of your rest;*
> *You and the ark of Your holiness.*
> *For the Lord has chosen Sion;*
> *He had desired it for His dwelling.*
> *This is my resting place forever,*
> *Here have I chosen to live.*

11

Modern Excavations

Archaeological excavations at Kiryat Yearim
Shmunis Family Excavations

With the permission of the Sisters of St. Joseph of the Apparition an archeological excavation began on their property in 2017. The findings have been amazing.

This ongoing dig has yielded evidence of a huge man-made shrine dating from 700–586 BC.

Excerpts from the "Times of Israel" 10 January 2019 follows:

A massive 8th century BC man-made platform discovered at a Catholic convent in central Israel may have served as an ancient shrine to the Ark of the Covenant, said leading Tel Aviv University archaeologist Israel Finkelstein....

Remains of the monumental, elevated podium have been unearthed on a Judean hilltop long associated with the location of biblical Kiriath-Jearim. According to the Hebrew Bible, the spot was the 80-year home of the Ark of the Covenant until taken by King David and paraded to Jerusalem.

Alongside some 50 student volunteers, in the summer of 2017 Finkelstein and co-directors Thomas Römer and Christophe Nicolle broke ground on the Shmunis Family Excavations at Kiriath-Jearim on the private grounds of a Catholic monastery situated near the central Israeli-Arab village of Abu Ghosh.

The archaeological dig is unusually located on private church property under the protection of the French government, a situation stemming from a 1949 agreement with the fledgling State of Israel. Today the site serves as the Convent of the (Mary) Ark of the Covenant, which covers the hill's summit, and is occupied by the Sisters of St. Joseph of the Apparition.

There is no possibility of excavating the summit, an important strategic location in the ancient world. "First, we cannot disturb the peace of the convent; second, the summit is probably eroded; third, it was built over by a large monastery in the Byzantine period," Finkelstein enumerated.

Even with the church construction, it is somewhat surprising that such an important biblical site has not yet been excavated. "Perhaps this has to do with the fact that it is a private property; certainly, one can understand the wish of the nuns not to be disturbed. Now, with the College de France involved, it was easier to get the green light from the convent," said Finkelstein.

In 1995-96, there was a small salvage excavation headed by Gabriel Barkay ahead of other convent construction on the hill. There were additional surveys conducted there by Amir Feldstein in the 1980s, and Boaz Zissu and Chris McKinny in 2013.

"The previous studies – both the salvage dig and the surveys – drew a similar picture of the settlement history of the site, but no find of note has been discovered," said Finkelstein.

That is, until the recent game-changing discovery of a massive man-made platform. The elevated rectangular podium, report the archaeologists, can be reconstructed to have been circa 150-110 meters (150 yards) in size and covering an area of some 1.65 hectares (4 acres). Created with typical Iron Age walls, 3-meters (10 feet) wide and which still stand 2-meter (6.5 feet) high, it is oriented exactly north-south and east-west.

Excavation of Kiriath Yearim
The Shmunis Family Excavations

Excavation at Kiriath Yearim - The Shmunis Family Excavations

12

Marian Prayers

Litany of Loreto

Lord, have mercy on us. R: Christ, have mercy on us.
Lord, have mercy on us. Christ hear us.
R: Christ, graciously hear us.
God, the Father in heaven,
R: Have mercy on us.
God, the Son, Redeemer of the world:,
R: Have mercy on us.
God, the Holy Ghost,
R: Have mercy on us.
Holy Trinity, One God,
R: Have mercy on us.
Holy Mary, R: pray for us.
Holy Mother of God, R: pray for us.
Holy Virgin of virgins, R: pray for us.
Mother of Christ, R: pray for us.

Mother of divine grace, R: pray for us.
Mother most pure, R: pray for us.
Mother most chaste, R: pray for us.
Mother inviolate, R: pray for us.
Mother undefiled, R: pray for us.
Mother most amiable, R: pray for us.
Mother most admirable, R: pray for us.
Mother of good counsel, R: pray for us.
Mother of our Creator, R: pray for us.
Mother of our Savior, R: pray for us.
Virgin most prudent, R: pray for us.
Virgin most venerable, R: pray for us.
Virgin most renowned, R: pray for us.
Virgin most powerful, R: pray for us.
Virgin most merciful, R: pray for us.
Virgin most faithful, R: pray for us.
Mirror of justice, R: pray for us.
Seat of wisdom, R: pray for us.
Cause of our joy, R: pray for us.
Spiritual vessel, R: pray for us.
Vessel of honor, R: pray for us.
Singular vessel of devotion, R: pray for us.
Mystical rose, R: pray for us.
Tower of David, R: pray for us.
Tower of ivory, R: pray for us.
House of gold, R: pray for us.
Ark of the covenant, R: pray for us.
Gate of Heaven, R: pray for us.
Morning star, R: pray for us.
Health of the sick, R: pray for us.
Refuge of sinners, R: pray for us.
Comforter of the afflicted, R: pray for us.

Help of Christians, R: pray for us.
Queen of angels, R: pray for us.
Queen of patriarchs, R: pray for us.
Queen of prophets, R: pray for us.
Queen of apostles, R: pray for us.
Queen of martyrs, R: pray for us.
Queen of confessors, R: pray for us.
Queen of virgins, R: pray for us.
Queen of all saints, R: pray for us.
Queen conceived without original sin, R: pray for us.
Queen assumed into heaven, R: pray for us.
Queen of the most holy Rosary, R: pray for us.
Queen of peace, R: pray for us.
Lamb of God, who takest away the sins of the world,
R: Spare us, O Lord.
Lamb of God, who takest away the sins of the world, R: Graciously hear us O Lord.
Lamb of God, who takest away the sins of the world, R: Have mercy on us.
V. Pray for us, O holy Mother of God
R. That we may be made worthy of the promises of Christ.

Let us pray:
Grant, O Lord God, we beseech Thee, that we Thy servants may rejoice in continual health of mind and body; and, through the glorious intercession of Blessed Mary ever Virgin, may be freed from present sorrow, and enjoy eternal gladness. Through Christ our Lord. Amen.

Marian Hymn

The Lord, Whom earth, and air, and sea
With one adoring voice resound,
Who rules them all with majesty;
In Mary's heart cloister found.

Lo! In a humble Virgin's womb,
Overshadowed by Almighty power;
He Whom the stars, and sun, and moon,
Each serve in their appointed hour.

O Mother blest! To whom was given
Within thy compass to contain
The Architect of Earth and Heaven,
Whose hands the universe sustain.

To thee was sent an Angel down;
In thee the Spirit was enshrined;
From thee came forth that Mighty One,
The long-desired of all mankind.

O Jesu! Born of Virgin bright,
Immortal glory be to Thee;
Praise to the Father Infinite,
And Holy Ghost eternally. Amen.

Mary the Dawn Hymn

Mary the dawn, Christ the Perfect Day;
Mary the gate, Christ the Heavenly Way!

Mary the root, Christ the Mystic Vine;
Mary the grape, Christ the Sacred Wine!

Mary the wheat, Christ the Living Bread;
Mary the rose tree, Christ the Rose blood-red!

Mary the font, Christ the Cleansing Flood;
Mary the cup, Christ the Saving Blood!

Mary the temple, Christ the temple's Lord;
Mary the shrine, Christ the God adored!

Mary the beacon, Christ the Haven's Rest;
Mary the mirror, Christ the Vision Blest!

Mary the mother, Christ the mother's Son
By all things blest while endless ages run.
Amen.

The Angelus

L. The Angel of the Lord declared unto Mary.
R. And she conceived of the Holy Spirit.

L. Hail Mary, full of grace, the Lord is with Thee;
Blessed art thou among women,
And blessed is the fruit of thy womb, Jesus.

R. Holy Mary, Mother of God,
Pray for us sinners,
now and at the hour of our death. Amen

L .Behold the handmaid of the Lord.
R. Be it done to me according to thy word.

Hail Mary...

L. And the Word was made flesh.
R. And dwelt among us.

Hail Mary...

L. Pray for us, O holy Mother of God.
R. That we may be made worthy of the promises of Christ.

Let us pray:
Pour forth, we beseech Thee, O Lord, Thy grace into our hearts, that we to whom the Incarnation of Christ Thy Son was made known by the message of an angel, may by His Passion and Cross be brought to the glory of His Resurrection. Through the same Christ Our Lord. Amen.

Hail Holy Queen

Hail, Holy Queen, Mother of Mercy,
our life, our sweetness and our hope.
To thee do we cry,
poor banished children of Eve.
To thee do we send up our sighs,
mourning and weeping in this valley of tears.
Turn then, most gracious advocate,
thine eyes of mercy toward us,
and after this our exile
show unto us the blessed fruit of thy womb, Jesus.
O clement, O loving,
O sweet Virgin Mary.

Lead: Pray for us, O holy Mother of God.
Response: That we may be made worthy of the promises of Christ.

The Regina Coeli

L. Queen of Heaven, rejoice,
R. Alleluia.
L. For the son whom you did merit to bear,
R. Alleluia.
L. Has risen as he said,
R. Alleluia.
L. Pray for us to God,
R. Alleluia.
L. Rejoice and be glad, O Virgin Mary,
R. Alleluia.

L For the Lord is truly risen,
R. Alleluia.

Let us pray:

O God, who gave joy to the world through the resurrection of thy Son, our Lord Jesus Christ, grant we beseech thee, that through the intercession of the Virgin Mary, His Mother, we may obtain the joys of everlasting life. Through the same Christ our Lord. Amen.

Memorare

Remember, O most gracious Virgin Mary,
that never was it known
that anyone who fled to thy protection,
implored thy help,
or sought thy intercession, was left unaided.
Inspired by this confidence
I fly unto thee, O Virgin of virgins, my Mother.
To thee do I come, before thee I kneel,
sinful and sorrowful.
O Mother of the Word Incarnate,
despise not my petitions, but in thy mercy hear and answer me.
Amen.

Magnificat

My soul proclaims the greatness of the Lord,
my spirit rejoices in God my Savior
for he has looked with favor on his lowly servant.
From this day all generations will call me blessed:
the Almighty has done great things for me,
and holy is his Name.
He has mercy on those who fear him
in every generation.
He has shown the strength of his arm,
he has scattered the proud in their conceit.
He has cast down the mighty from their thrones,
and has lifted up the lowly.
He has filled the hungry with good things,
and the rich he has sent away empty.
He has come to the help of his servant Israel
for he has remembered his promise of mercy,
the promise he made to our fathers,
to Abraham and his children for ever.
Glory to the Father, and to the Son,
and to the Holy Spirit:
as it was in the beginning, is now,
and will be for ever. Amen.

Sing of Mary

Sing of Mary, pure and lowly,
Virgin mother undefiled,
Sing of God's own Son most holy,
Who became her little child.

Fairest child of fairest mother,
God the Lord who came to earth,
Word made flesh, our very brother,
Takes our nature by his birth.

Sing of Jesus, son of Mary,
In the home at Nazareth.
Toil and labor cannot weary
Love enduring unto death.

Constant was the love he gave her,
Though he went forth from her side,
Forth to preach, and heal, and suffer,
Till on Calvary he died.

Glory be to God the Father;
Glory be to God the Son;
Glory be to God the Spirit;
Glory to the Three in One.

From the heart of blessed Mary,
From all saints the song ascends,
And the Church the strain reechoes
Unto earth's remotest ends.

End Notes

Chapters 10 and 11 were taken directly from the Sisters of Saint Jospeh of the Apparition booklet on Sister Josephine entitled "Sr. Josephine and the Ark" no publication date available. The only "author" cited is Rev. Fr. Gerry O'Hara O.M.I.

ABOUT THE AUTHOR

Barbara Gaskell is the foundress and director of the Mother Angelica Museum in Canton, Ohio. In 1989 she began St. Raphael Bookstore in a 300 square foot office space. Today St. Raphael Center is a 7500 square foot facility that houses a gift shop, chapel, studio for the Living Bread Radio Network, Mother Angelica Museum, outdoor rosary garden and Lourdes grotto. Barbara's life is dedicated to spreading the Good News of Jesus Christ.

OTHER BOOKS BY THE AUTHOR

The Amazing Life of Rita Rizzo: The Early Years of Mother Mary Angelica

The Mother Angelica Tour Prayerbook